UNDERSEA
CREATURES

KINGFISHER
LONDON & NEW YORK

Published in the United States by Kingfisher,
175 Fifth Ave., New York, NY 10010
Kingfisher is an imprint of Macmillan Children's Books, London.
All rights reserved.

Distributed in the U.S. and Canada by Macmillan,
175 Fifth Ave., New York, NY 10010

WELDON OWEN INC.
CEO, President Terry Newell
VP, Sales and New Business Development Amy Kaneko

VP, Publisher Roger Shaw
Executive Editor Mariah Bear
Editor Lucie Parker
Project Editors Nam Nguyen, Sarah Hines Stephens
Editorial Assistant Emelie Griffin

Associate Creative Director Kelly Booth
Senior Designer William Mack
Assistant Designer Michel Gadwa

Production Director Chris Hemesath
Production Manager Michelle Duggan
Color Manager Teri Bell

Library of Congress Cataloging-in-Publication data has been applied for.

ISBN:978-0-7534-6666-7

Kingfisher books are available for special promotions and premiums.
For details contact: Special Markets Department, Macmillan, 175 Fifth Ave., New York, NY 10010.

For more information, please visit www.kingfisherbooks.com

A Weldon Owen Production
415 Jackson Street
San Francisco, California 94111

Printed in Shenzhen, China, by Asia Pacific Offset.
5 4 3 2
2011 2012 2013 2014 2015

UNDERSEA
CREATURES

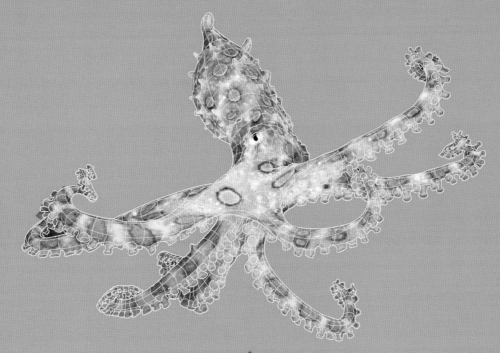

KINGFISHER

NEW YORK

CONTENTS

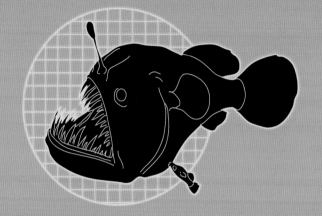

MEET THE BEASTS

Earth is a water planet—almost two-thirds of it is covered by ocean—and while a sliver of life exists on land, the majority of the planet's population thrives in the seas. Splashing in the shallows, clinging to reefs, and lurking in the depths are multitudes of fantastic creatures, each one specially equipped for life underwater. Internal lights help dwellers of the deep seas pierce through the darkness. Regenerating teeth keep hunters armed and sharp. Color-changing abilities and swiveling eyes help vulnerable animals spot danger before it spots them. What other fascinating tools and tricks does it take to swim in this extremely crowded, high-pressure, and watery world? Dive in and discover!

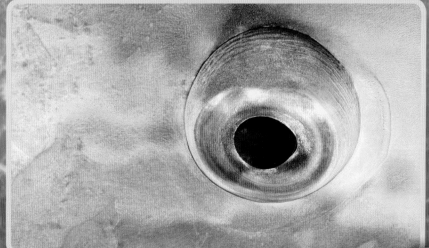

CLOAK AND DAGGERS

Lionfish like to swim lazily in open waters with their fins spread like delicate lace. They may look frail, but their appearance is only a cover for some vicious capabilities—lionfish float fearlessly inside a coat of concealed weapons. Beneath their camouflaged fins hide nineteen venomous spines that can inflict intense pain and deliver tissue-destroying poison.

GEOGRAPHY
Red Sea, Indian Ocean, South Pacific Ocean, coasts of China and Japan

HABITAT
Swims near coral reefs and rocky crevices

LIONFISH
Pterois volitans

LENGTH: **11 INCHES (28 CM)**   WEIGHT: **1 POUND (0.5 KG)**

INTELLIGENCE
■■■■■■□□□□□

AGILITY
■■■■■■■■■□□

STRENGTH
■■■□□□□□□□□

ENDURANCE
■■■■■■■□□□□

SPEED
■■■■□□□□□□□

DEFENSE
■■■■■■■□□□□

PREY

FISH
Lionfish suck up small fish and crustaceans. By moving slowly and blending in with the coral, they catch their prey unaware.

TOOL TIME

SPINE-RAISING
When threatened or defending their territory, lionfish erect all of their spines, presenting a full radius of sharp spikes and putting their enemies in a very prickly position.

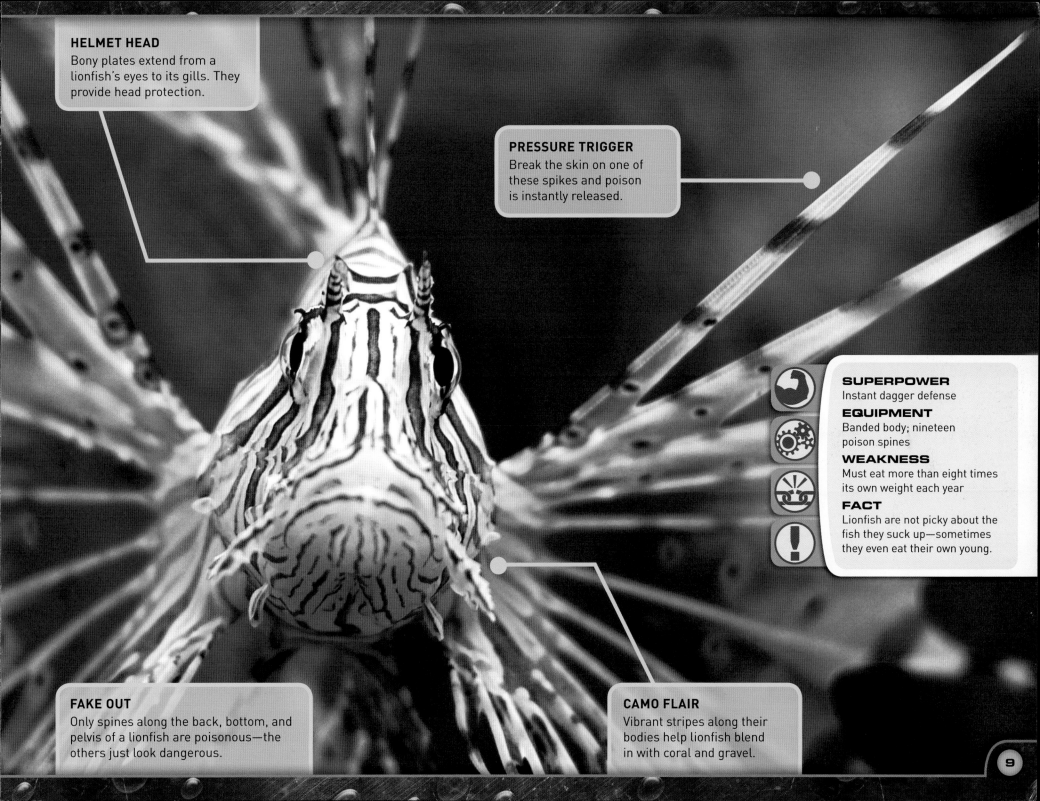

HELMET HEAD
Bony plates extend from a lionfish's eyes to its gills. They provide head protection.

PRESSURE TRIGGER
Break the skin on one of these spikes and poison is instantly released.

SUPERPOWER
Instant dagger defense

EQUIPMENT
Banded body; nineteen poison spines

WEAKNESS
Must eat more than eight times its own weight each year

FACT
Lionfish are not picky about the fish they suck up—sometimes they even eat their own young.

FAKE OUT
Only spines along the back, bottom, and pelvis of a lionfish are poisonous—the others just look dangerous.

CAMO FLAIR
Vibrant stripes along their bodies help lionfish blend in with coral and gravel.

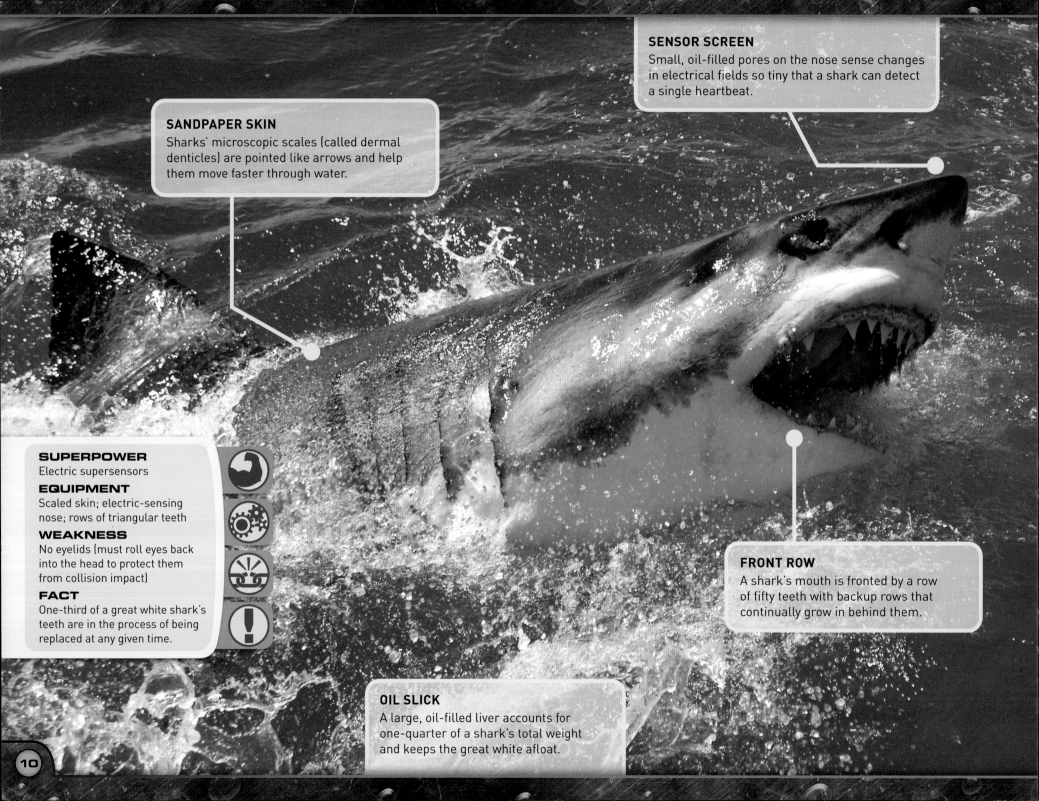

SENSOR SCREEN
Small, oil-filled pores on the nose sense changes in electrical fields so tiny that a shark can detect a single heartbeat.

SANDPAPER SKIN
Sharks' microscopic scales (called dermal denticles) are pointed like arrows and help them move faster through water.

SUPERPOWER
Electric supersensors

EQUIPMENT
Scaled skin; electric-sensing nose; rows of triangular teeth

WEAKNESS
No eyelids (must roll eyes back into the head to protect them from collision impact)

FACT
One-third of a great white shark's teeth are in the process of being replaced at any given time.

FRONT ROW
A shark's mouth is fronted by a row of fifty teeth with backup rows that continually grow in behind them.

OIL SLICK
A large, oil-filled liver accounts for one-quarter of a shark's total weight and keeps the great white afloat.

GEOGRAPHY
Worldwide, especially coastal waters of South Africa and New Zealand

HABITAT
Circles in coastal and open temperate waters

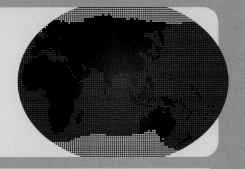

JAWS OF DEATH
Great white sharks are supreme predators—they can track enormous prey weighing up to 1 ton (0.9 tonne). Their reputation as people-eaters, however, is undeserved: While these massive sharks do attack people, great whites rarely eat them. Sharks mistake humans for prey, attack, and then leave. Death occurs due to trauma and blood loss.

ALLY

REMORAS
Remoras latch onto the sides of great whites with special suction dorsal fins. They enjoy the free transportation—and the free leftovers.

PREY

SEALS
Great whites are especially fond of seals. These sharks can bite the heads off huge elephant seals weighing up to 1,000 pounds (450 kg) each.

RAYS
There's nothing quite like family, and great white sharks love to have their cousins—such as stingrays, bat rays, and skates—for dinner!

SEA TURTLES
The hard, protective shells of sea turtles are no match for a great white's jaws. Sharks munch on delicious fatty turtle sandwiches.

GREAT WHITE SHARK
Carcharodon carcharias

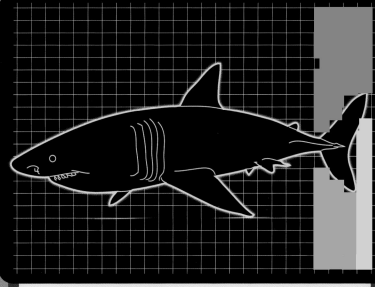

LENGTH: **19 FEET (5.75 M)**   WEIGHT: **3 TONS (2.75 TONNES)**

INTELLIGENCE
■■■■■■■■■□

AGILITY
■■■■■■■■□

STRENGTH
■■■■■■■■■■

ENDURANCE
■■■■■■■■■□

SPEED
■■■■■■■■■□

ATTACK
■■■■■■■■■■

SEA SERPENT

In spite of the fact that they have lungs and breathe air, banded sea kraits spend most of their lives in water and come up on land only to lay eggs. Another trait they share with their land-dwelling relations is their deadly venom. Kraits' poison is similar to cobras', is just as lethal, and even keeps the sea snakes safe: they're so poisonous, nothing likes to eat them!

GEOGRAPHY
Coasts of Southeast Asia, Indonesia, Pacific Islands

HABITAT
Slithers through mangroves and around coral islands and reefs

BANDED SEA KRAIT
Laticauda colubrina

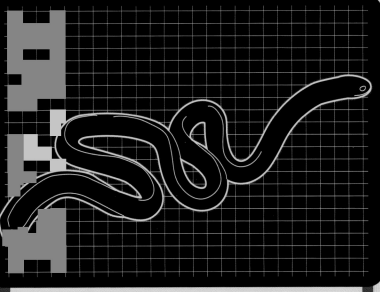

LENGTH: **3 FEET (1 M)**   WEIGHT: **4.5 POUNDS (2 KG)**

INTELLIGENCE	AGILITY
■■■■■■□■■□	■■■■■■■■□■□

STRENGTH	ENDURANCE
■■■■□■■■□	■■■■■□■■■□

SPEED	EVASION
■■■■■■□■□	■■■■■■■■□□

PREY

EELS
Sea kraits attack eels so often that some have built up a tolerance to snake poison. But even resistant eels will die after repeated bites.

TOOL TIME

FLAT FEET
Sea kraits swim the same way that snakes move on land—by slithering. Unlike land snakes, kraits have flattened tails that work like paddles in the water for both steering and propulsion.

TAIL LIGHT
Krait tails are light sensitive, so they can keep an "eye" out for danger even if their heads are hidden deep in crevices.

OXYGEN TANK
By squeezing air from extra, dormant lungs, sea snakes can breathe longer during deep dives.

NOSE PLUG
Sea krait nostrils can expand to seal out water and retract to let in air.

SUPER ABSORPTION
During long dives, gill-less sea kraits absorb oxygen in water through their skin.

SUPERPOWERS
Enhanced oxygen intake; amphibious ability

EQUIPMENT
Two poisonous fangs; long body; flattened paddle tail

WEAKNESS
Must lay eggs on land

FACT
Sea kraits stick out their tongues to detect scents and spit out salt.

ESCAPE MECHANISM
With no bones at all, an octopus can squeeze into an opening as small as its own beak.

SMOKE SCREEN
When threatened, octopuses release ink clouds. The "screen" confuses predators while octopuses slip away.

STEALTH TECHNOLOGY
Octopuses are able to change both their skin color and texture to blend in with their surroundings.

SUPERPOWER
Morphing skills

EQUIPMENT
Eight detachable arms; strong suckers; three hearts

WEAKNESS
Weak blood (can't hold much oxygen)

FACT
The giant Pacific octopus weighs up to 600 pounds (270 kg).

SENSORY OVERLOAD
Octopus tentacles do triple duty: touching, grasping, and even tasting.

GEOGRAPHY
Tropical and subtropical coasts worldwide

HABITAT
Squeezes through rocky reefs

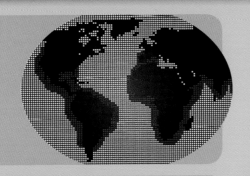

ESCAPE ARTIST

Smart, strong, and stealthy, octopuses have lots of tricks up their eight sleeves. Evasion techniques include detachable arms and the ability to change their appearance to fade into the background or warn off enemies. In addition, they are armed with lightning-fast tentacles that respond and grab prey reflexively, making these predators adept at hiding and hunting.

PREY

CRAYFISH
Small, shrimplike crayfish don't stand a chance against an octopus's eight muscular and sneaky tentacles.

ENEMIES

DOLPHINS
With lightning speed and incredible intelligence, dolphins are both nimble and clever enough to corner wily octopuses.

EELS
An eel waiting in the cracks of a rock or reef is a nasty surprise for an octopus looking for a place to hide.

SHARKS
The sea is a shark's buffet, and they are always on the lookout for a boneless snack of tasty tentacles.

COMMON OCTOPUS
Octopus vulgaris

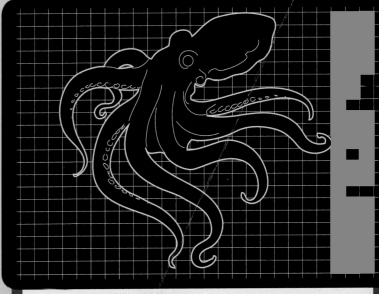

LENGTH: **3 FEET (1 M)** WEIGHT: **8.75 POUNDS (4 KG)**

INTELLIGENCE
■■■■■■■■■

AGILITY
■■■■■■■■■

STRENGTH
■■■■■■■■■

ENDURANCE
■■■■■■■■■

SPEED
■■■■■■■■■

EVASION
■■■■■■■■■

JOURNEY TO THE DEEP

The sea is divided into zones by depth. Most ocean life exists near the surface, where sunlight makes plant life abundant. Extreme survivors emerge in the deepest depths where they deal with total darkness, frigid temperatures, scarce food supplies, and bone-crushing water pressure.

VESSEL: **DEEP ROVER**
YEAR MADE: **1984**
MAX DEPTH: **1,000 FEET (300 M)**

OCEAN LEVELS

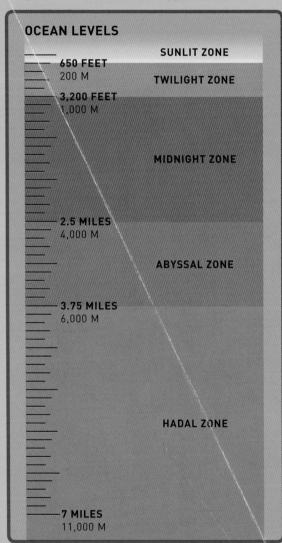

	SUNLIT ZONE
650 FEET 200 M	TWILIGHT ZONE
3,200 FEET 1,000 M	
	MIDNIGHT ZONE
2.5 MILES 4,000 M	
	ABYSSAL ZONE
3.75 MILES 6,000 M	
	HADAL ZONE
7 MILES 11,000 M	

PLUNGING THE DEPTHS

Humans have descended 7 miles (11 km) into the Mariana Trench, the deepest known part of the ocean. It is found off the Pacific coast of Asia.

OCTOPUSES

CLOWN FISH

SUNLIT ZONE

Most ocean animals live at depths of 0 to 650 feet (0–200 m). Light filters to these waters, supplying energy for algae—the base of the food chain that feeds sharks (above), clown fish, and octopuses.

VESSEL: BATHYSPHERE
YEAR MADE: **1934**
MAX DEPTH: **2,950 FEET (900 M)**

DEEP DIVING

In 1934, William Beebe and Otis Barton created a bathysphere—a steel ball suspended from a cable—to explore the ocean depths. Since then, advances in technology have allowed scientists to venture far deeper. Modern submersibles withstand pressure 680 times greater than sea level, insulate passengers from frigid temperatures, and house life-support systems for one to three passengers.

VESSEL: SHINKAI 6500
YEAR MADE: **1990**
MAX DEPTH: **21,325 FEET (6,500 M)**

TWILIGHT ZONE

Cnidarians (above), red spider crabs, and sea urchins live 650 to 3,200 feet (200–1,000 m) below the waves. To avoid predators, the twilight dwellers rise to feed in the sunlit zone in the evenings.

RED SPIDER CRABS

SEA URCHINS

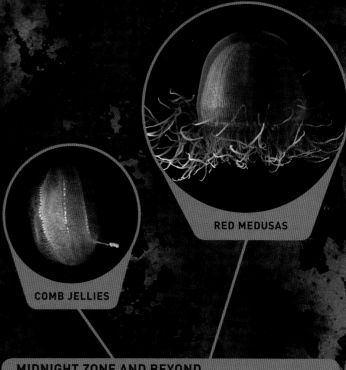

RED MEDUSAS

COMB JELLIES

MIDNIGHT ZONE AND BEYOND

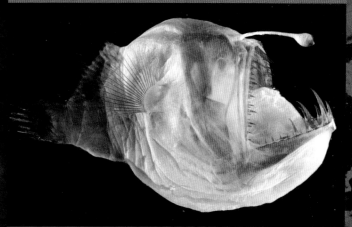

Blackdevil anglerfish (above), comb jellies, and red medusas survive in the pitch-black, high-pressure deep ocean that begins at 3,200 feet (1,000 m) deep. They're aided by a host of bizarre adaptations, such as glowing organs and expandable bodies and jaws.

DARK ILLUSIONIST

In the cold, dark, and high-pressure reaches of the deep sea, survival of the fittest doesn't entail being the biggest or fastest. The trick is finding food, and female anglerfish have developed a technique that allows them to eat and save energy. Instead of tracking down prey, they lure unsuspecting fish to their waiting jaws by dangling bioluminescent lights in the darkness.

GEOGRAPHY
Tropical and temperate waters worldwide

HABITAT
Hovers between 3,200 and 13,000 feet (1,000–4,000 m)

BLACKDEVIL ANGLERFISH
Melanocetus johnsoni

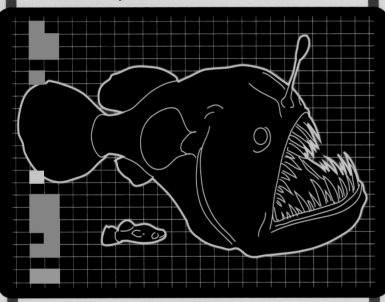

LENGTH (FEMALE): **5 INCHES (13 CM)** LENGTH (MALE): **1 INCH (2.5 CM)**

INTELLIGENCE

AGILITY

STRENGTH

ENDURANCE

SPEED

ATTACK

MEAL TICKET
Male and female anglerfish look very different from each other. Females are much larger and have hunting lures. Tiny males seek out females and attach themselves to their sides, sometimes for life. The males depend on their large mates for food.

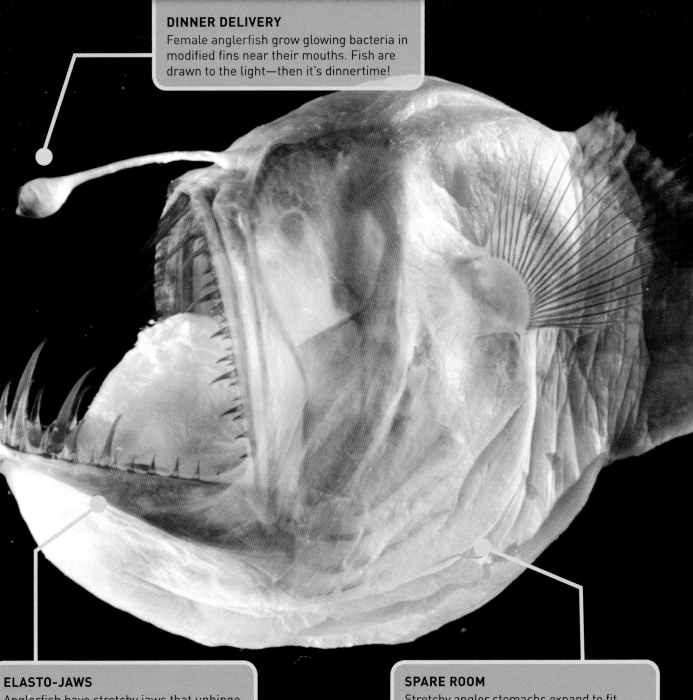

DINNER DELIVERY
Female anglerfish grow glowing bacteria in modified fins near their mouths. Fish are drawn to the light—then it's dinnertime!

HAIR WAVES
The long, hairlike tendrils on top of anglerfish heads sense both sound and movement.

SUPERPOWER
Irresistible illumination

EQUIPMENT
Large gaping jaw; glowing lure; expandable stomach

WEAKNESS
Poor swimmer (anglerfish wobble when they swim)

FACT
Male anglerfish use their giant nose organs to sniff out females.

ELASTO-JAWS
Anglerfish have stretchy jaws that unhinge to open wide. They can swallow animals larger than their own heads!

SPARE ROOM
Stretchy angler stomachs expand to fit supersize meals. Anglers slowly digest big prey over long periods of time.

SUPERPOWER
Ultimate camouflage

EQUIPMENT
Leaflike appendages; armor plates; prickly spines

WEAKNESS
No stomach (must eat constantly or will starve to death)

FACT
Sea dragons live off the coast of Australia and nowhere else.

HEAD-MOUNTED STEERING
Leafy tentacles are just for looks. Sea dragons navigate with tiny fins found on their heads.

PRECISION TARGETING
By swiveling independently of one another, sea dragon eyes can home in on two different prey at the same time.

COOL CAMOUFLAGE
Sea dragons' thin appendages closely resemble kelp, which keeps them hidden in their sea-grass beds.

SUPER SIPPER
Sea dragons have fused jaws that don't open and close. They work like straws for sucking up krill.

GEOGRAPHY
Southern coast of Australia

HABITAT
Hides in kelp reefs and sheltered sea-grass beds

MASTER OF DISGUISE

Draped in colorful ribbons and shaped unlike any other creature in the ocean, sea dragons are strikingly distinctive. However, you'd be hard pressed to find them when they are hidden within grass and coral. These creatures' ability to change color and blend into their surroundings provides them with an almost perfect invisibility cloak.

LIFE OR DEATH

DADDY DAYCARE
Like sea horses (above), sea dragon daddies incubate eggs laid by females. Sea horses hold eggs in front pouches, but sea dragons incubate them tucked partway inside the skin of their tails.

LEAFY SEA DRAGON
Phycodurus eques

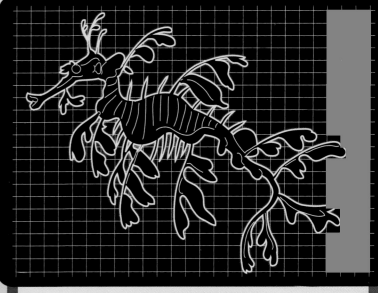

LENGTH: **12 INCHES (30 CM)**

INTELLIGENCE
■■■■□□□□□□

AGILITY
■■■■■■□□□□

STRENGTH
■■■□□□□□□□

ENDURANCE
■■■■□□□□□□

SPEED
■■■■■□□□□□

EVASION
■■■■■■■□□□

POWER PUFF

Salmon will spit out puffer fish rather than swallow them. Even large fish called groupers will let themselves starve before eating puffers. These predators avoid the prickly fish in part because they inflate when threatened, but the real reason is that puffer fish are extremely poisonous. Many big fish can taste a puffer's toxins, which can cause paralysis and death.

GEOGRAPHY
Indo-Pacific, Pacific Ocean, Gulf of Mexico, Atlantic Ocean along Florida and Venezuela coasts

HABITAT
Inflates in temperate salty or brackish waters

WHITE-SPOTTED PUFFER FISH *Arothron hispidus*

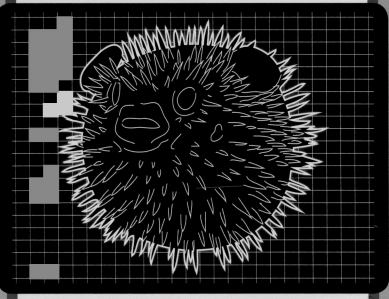

LENGTH: **1 INCH (2.5 CM)**   WEIGHT: **0.05 OUNCES (1.5 G)**

INTELLIGENCE
■■■■■□□□□□

AGILITY
■■■■□□□□□□

STRENGTH
■■■■□□□□□□

ENDURANCE
■■■■□□□□□□

SPEED
■■■□□□□□□□

DEFENSE
■■■■■■□□□□

IN ACTION

PUFF BALL
Some puffer fish have prickly skin and balloon into sharp, pointy spheres when threatened. Puffer fish inflate by filling their stomachs with water, making their spines spike out. Their normally small stomachs have folds within folds that allow them to expand to nearly a hundred times their original size!

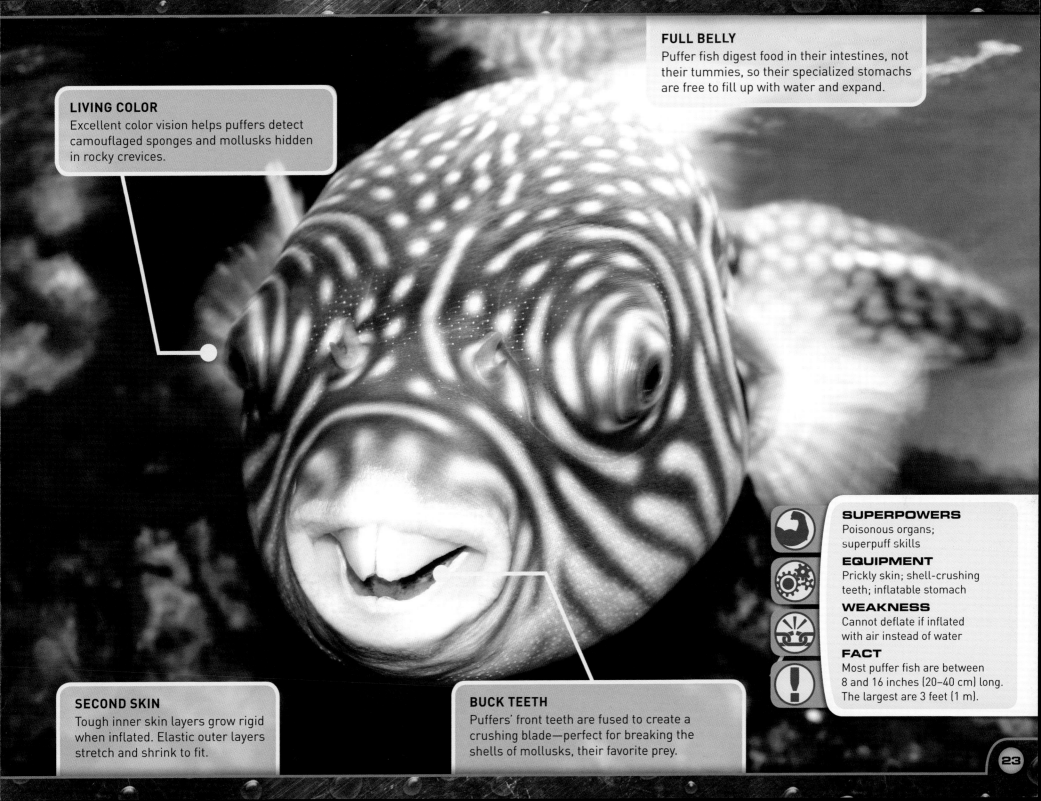

FULL BELLY
Puffer fish digest food in their intestines, not their tummies, so their specialized stomachs are free to fill up with water and expand.

LIVING COLOR
Excellent color vision helps puffers detect camouflaged sponges and mollusks hidden in rocky crevices.

SUPERPOWERS
Poisonous organs; superpuff skills

EQUIPMENT
Prickly skin; shell-crushing teeth; inflatable stomach

WEAKNESS
Cannot deflate if inflated with air instead of water

FACT
Most puffer fish are between 8 and 16 inches (20–40 cm) long. The largest are 3 feet (1 m).

SECOND SKIN
Tough inner skin layers grow rigid when inflated. Elastic outer layers stretch and shrink to fit.

BUCK TEETH
Puffers' front teeth are fused to create a crushing blade—perfect for breaking the shells of mollusks, their favorite prey.

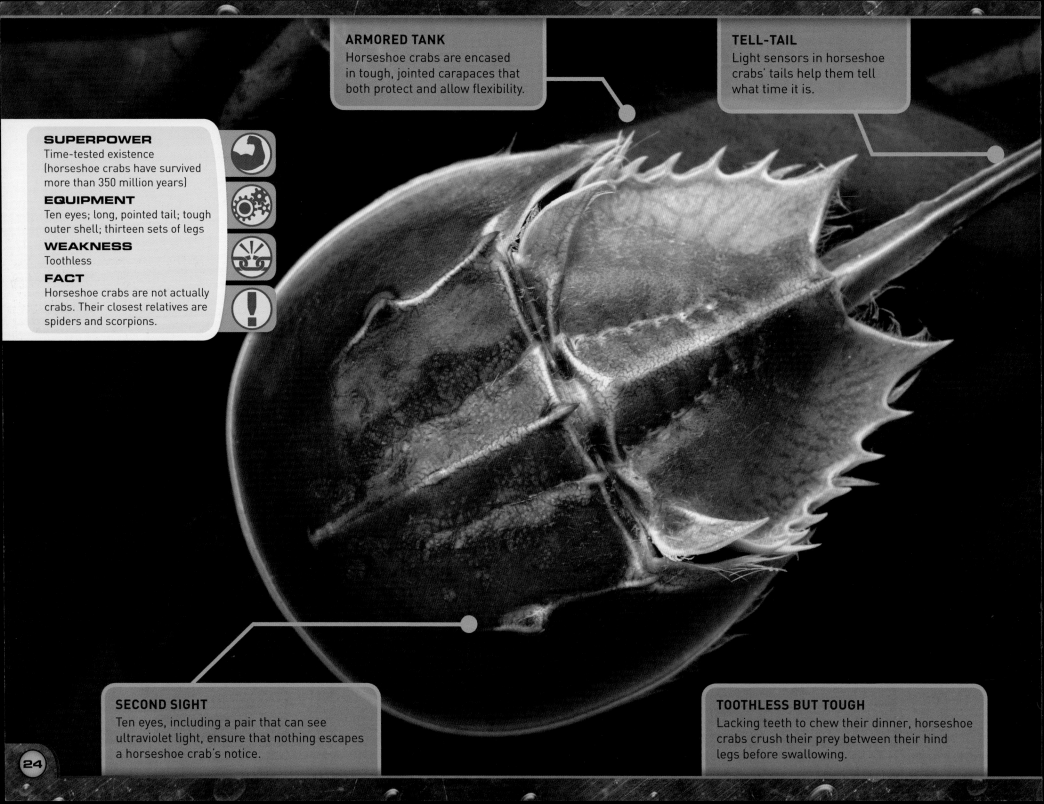

ARMORED TANK
Horseshoe crabs are encased in tough, jointed carapaces that both protect and allow flexibility.

TELL-TAIL
Light sensors in horseshoe crabs' tails help them tell what time it is.

SUPERPOWER
Time-tested existence (horseshoe crabs have survived more than 350 million years)

EQUIPMENT
Ten eyes; long, pointed tail; tough outer shell; thirteen sets of legs

WEAKNESS
Toothless

FACT
Horseshoe crabs are not actually crabs. Their closest relatives are spiders and scorpions.

SECOND SIGHT
Ten eyes, including a pair that can see ultraviolet light, ensure that nothing escapes a horseshoe crab's notice.

TOOTHLESS BUT TOUGH
Lacking teeth to chew their dinner, horseshoe crabs crush their prey between their hind legs before swallowing.

GEOGRAPHY

Atlantic coastal waters from Nova Scotia to the Yucatán; Gulf of Mexico

HABITAT

Sweeps through shallow water over sandy or muddy seabeds

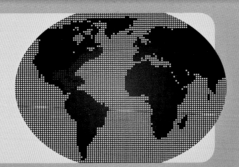

HARD-SHELLED HEALER

They look like armored pods and are equipped with foaming blue blood and a terrifying array of jointed legs beneath their smooth shells. As alien as they seem, horseshoe crabs have outlived dinosaurs. Their valuable blood is used to detect bacteria in vaccines before they are made available to the public. A quart of the precious liquid sells for more than a car.

PREY

MOLLUSKS

These prehistoric crawlers love mollusks (such as common clams). They also dine on algae, and worms that live on seabeds.

HORSESHOE CRAB
Limulus polyphemus

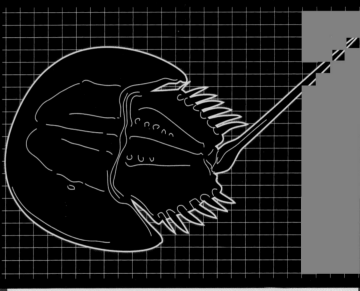

LENGTH: **2 FEET (60 CM)**   WEIGHT: **3 POUNDS (1.5 KG)**

TOOL TIME

POLE VAULT

Unlike turtles, horseshoe crabs will not die if turned on their backs. They dig their long tails, called telsons, into the sand and use them like levers to flip themselves back onto their feet.

INTELLIGENCE	AGILITY
■■■■■□□□□□	■■■■■□□□□□

STRENGTH	ENDURANCE
■■■■■■□□□□	■■■■■■■■□□

SPEED	DEFENSE
■■■■■■■□□□	■■■■■■■■□□

DEEP TROUBLE

Leopard seals are deceptively cute. But the spotted coats that inspire their name are a clue to these sea killers' awesome predatory skills. Weighing more than half a ton (more than 455 kg), these arctic hunters are the second-largest seal species after giant elephant seals. They slice speedily through icy waters and eat whatever they want, including other seals.

GEOGRAPHY
Southern Ocean

HABITAT
Hunts on ice and in freezing waters

LEOPARD SEAL
Hydrurga leptonyx

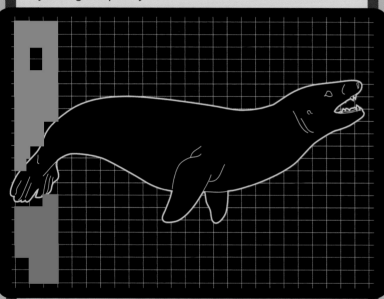

LENGTH: **12 FEET (3.5 M)**   WEIGHT: **1,200 POUNDS (545 KG)**

INTELLIGENCE
■■■■■■■□■■

AGILITY
■■■■■■■■□■

STRENGTH
■■■■■■■□■■

ENDURANCE
■■■■■■■□■■

SPEED
■■■■■■□■■■

ATTACK
■■■■■■■■■■

ENEMY

KILLER WHALES
Huge leopard seals have little to fear on the ice, but stealthy killer whales wait near beaches and at the edge of ice to catch seals in their toothy jaws.

PREY

PENGUINS
Slow, waddling Adélie penguins don't stand a chance against fast and fearsome leopard seals on land or in the water.

FUR SEALS
Leopard seals show no favors toward family. They are known for viciously hunting other seals, such as their cousins, fur seals.

SQUID
Versatile leopard seals go for smaller prey as well, chewing up squid like calamari snacks.

RATHER SHALLOW

Not known for diving—other seal species fare better—leopard seals can still dive as deep as 1,395 feet (425 m) and stay submerged for almost ten minutes.

PERILOUS PERISCOPE

Leopard seals wait for their prey, lurking just beneath the water's surface with only their eyes and self-sealing nostrils peeking out.

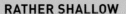

SUPERPOWER
Superior hunting skills

EQUIPMENT
Sleek, torpedo-shaped body; massive jaws; large size

WEAKNESS
Poor air supply (can't store as much oxygen as other seals)

FACT
Leopard seals don't have visible ears. Their ears are internal, with only a pinhole opening.

BED HEAD

Leopard seals don't have bad hair days. Their fur stays pressed close to their skin to seal out water.

FAT COAT

A thick layer of blubber insulates leopard seals from frigid water temperatures as cold as 28°F (–2°C).

GEOGRAPHY
Tropical Atlantic Ocean, Mediterranean Sea

HABITAT
Floats on the surfaces of tropical and subtropical waters

AIR BALLOON
Man-of-war floats contain up to 1 quart (1 l) of gas. They deflate to descend and inflate to rise to the surface.

SPAGHETTI FEED
Specialized polyps on the underside of the float, where the tendrils meet, digest food for the entire colony.

HITCHING A RIDE
Some fish, such as clown fish, are immune to the man-of-war's tentacles. These fish often swim among the stingers, shielding themselves against predators.

BARBED WIRES

Each man-of-war tendril is about 33 feet (10 m) long and has the ability to inflict multiple stings.

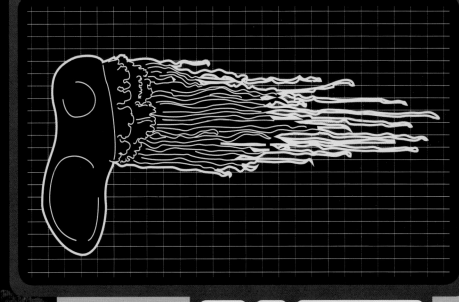

SUPERPOWERS

Teamwork; superspecialization

EQUIPMENT

Gas-filled float; many coiled tendrils; stinging cells

WEAKNESS

Soft body (easily damaged in storms)

FACT

Man-of-war stings are extremely painful and can even cause heart failure!

THE STING

Often mistaken for jellyfish, Portuguese man-of-wars are actually colonies of four different types of polyps—each type with its own job—living together. Beautiful blue or purple floats inflate to take the group up and down while other polyps hanging below gather and process food or offer protection in the form of heart-stopping stings.

PORTUGUESE MAN-OF-WAR

Physalia physalis

LENGTH: 38 FEET (11.5 M)   HEIGHT (FLOAT): 13 INCHES (33 CM)

INTELLIGENCE

STRENGTH

SPEED

AGILITY

ENDURANCE

ATTACK

PRICKLY SITUATION

Crown-of-thorns sea stars get their name from the thin spines that cover them, each of which can grow as long as 3 inches (7.5 cm)—about as tall as an apple. Although being skewered is a real pain, it's the slimy surface of the spine that's dangerous: the slippery coating is poisonous, and a single prick may cause swelling, numbness, nausea, vomiting, or paralysis.

GEOGRAPHY
Indo-Pacific region, Australian coastal waters

HABITAT
Crawls along the bottom of seabeds and coral reefs

PREY

CORAL POLYPS
Crown-of-thorns like to gnaw on coral polyps. Periodic sea-star population explosions create large sections of stripped reefs.

CROWN-OF-THORNS SEA STAR *Acanthaster planci*

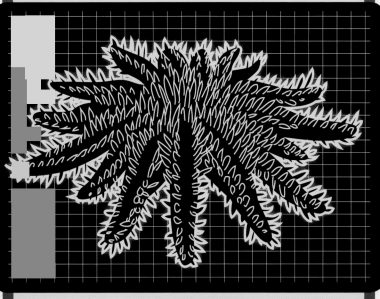

LENGTH: **2 FEET (60 CM)**

INTELLIGENCE
■■■■■■■■■■

AGILITY
■■■■■■■■■■

STRENGTH
■■■■■■■■■■

ENDURANCE
■■■■■■■■■■

SPEED
■■■■■■■■■■

ATTACK
■■■■■■■■■■

IN ACTION

OUT TO EAT
Sea stars get their meals by pushing their stomachs outside of their bodies to surround their prey. Then dissolving chemicals turn their food into a soupy mix that sea stars absorb before retracting their guts.

WATER PUMPS
Sea stars use water (not blood) to circulate oxygen inside their bodies and also to inflate their tube feet.

ROCK STAR
Calcium in sea-star skin makes it hard to the touch and adds a layer of protection.

BACKUP COPY
Detached along with a bit of body, one leg can regenerate an entire sea star.

SUPERPOWER
Self-regeneration

EQUIPMENT
Thirteen to sixteen arms; tube feet; calcified skin; poisonous, slime-covered spines

WEAKNESS
Lacks eyes and a brain

FACT
The crown-of-thorns is the only known poisonous sea star.

MULTIPURPOSE DEVICE
Sea stars use their tube feet to move, breathe, search for prey, and urinate.

LIFE ON THE REEF

Coral reefs form in clear, tropical waters where there is a lack of phytoplankton—the base of most ocean food webs. The entire reef ecosystem depends instead on algae living inside coral. Using algae's solar energy, coral build incredible reef homes that provide neighborhoods and hunting grounds for all. In return, each reef inhabitant contributes to maintaining these unique communities.

REEF GRAZING

Nudibranchs (sea slugs) eat sea sponges and anemones. By preying on animals that eat coral, nudibranchs ensure that not too much of the reef is eaten away.

REST STOP

Green sea turtles travel great distances and depend on reefs to refuel on food. Though they are brown, turtles' diets of algae and sea grass turn their insides green.

FOR RENT

Mantis shrimp have powerful claws that they use to catch prey and burrow. Abandoned shrimp passageways make homes for other animals.

CLEANING STATION

Some reef animals have devised clever ways to earn their living—they set up shop. This coral shrimp runs a cleaning station, eating parasites and dead skin from other animals. Fish line up to wait for the shrimp's special services.

STONE SOUP

Parrotfish add to the landscaping by nibbling algae from the surface of the reef, often tearing off whole chunks. These hard coral pieces are then broken down inside fish and expelled as sand. A single parrotfish can contribute up to 198 pounds (90 kg) of sand a year.

SPLIT SECONDS
These speedy predators capture and swallow their food in less than a minute.

JAW EXTENSIONS
A second set of jaws in the moray's throat can extend into the mouth to hold wriggling prey.

SUPERPOWERS
Stealth hunting; slime protection

EQUIPMENT
Sharp teeth; streamlined body; extra jaws

WEAKNESS
No protective scales

FACT
Toxins present in eel stomachs, intestines, and livers attack the red blood cells of humans.

HASTY HEALING
Moray eels have been known to heal from bone-exposing injuries within a few days, without scarring.

SLIME ATTACK
When captured, eels secrete a slimy substance from their skin to aid in slippery escapes.

STONE SOUP

Parrotfish add to the landscaping by nibbling algae from the surface of the reef, often tearing off whole chunks. These hard coral pieces are then broken down inside fish and expelled as sand. A single parrotfish can contribute up to 198 pounds (90 kg) of sand a year.

ANIMAL, VEGETABLE, OR MINERAL?

Coral are animals that start life as soft-bodied polyps that collect algae by eating it. Storing algae inside their bodies, coral cluster together to form colonies and build large, rocklike structures (reefs). Their dazzling mineral houses serve to protect the coral and keep precious algae near the sunlit surface. Algae require sunlight to make food the way other plants do—through photosynthesis. Competition for space and light lead to coral's fantastic shape and color variations.

SPLIT SECONDS
These speedy predators capture and swallow their food in less than a minute.

JAW EXTENSIONS
A second set of jaws in the moray's throat can extend into the mouth to hold wriggling prey.

SUPERPOWERS
Stealth hunting; slime protection

EQUIPMENT
Sharp teeth; streamlined body; extra jaws

WEAKNESS
No protective scales

FACT
Toxins present in eel stomachs, intestines, and livers attack the red blood cells of humans.

HASTY HEALING
Moray eels have been known to heal from bone-exposing injuries within a few days, without scarring.

SLIME ATTACK
When captured, eels secrete a slimy substance from their skin to aid in slippery escapes.

Giant moray eels live up to their name, stretching longer than the average human is tall. By hiding their length in the nooks and shadows of coral reefs and emerging mainly at night, these sharp-toothed stalkers have snatched many an unsuspecting beast and the occasional human hand! Morays are such good hunters that other animals recruit them to help.

GEOGRAPHY
Red Sea, Indian Ocean, South Pacific Ocean

HABITAT
Lurks in tropical reef crevices

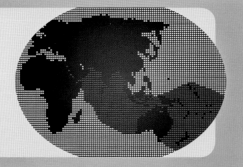

PREY

REEF FISH
Eels weave through the cracks and crevices of coral reefs looking for hidden fish and crunchy crustaceans.

ALLY

DOUBLE TEAM
In the Red Sea, groupers team up with giant moray eels to hunt for food. The eels guard reef nooks while the groupers stalk nearby open waters, leaving prey no place to hide.

GIANT MORAY EEL
Gymnothorax javanicus

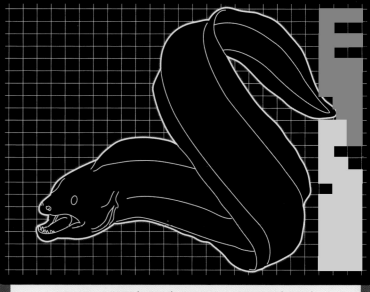

LENGTH: **9 FEET (2.75 M)**   WEIGHT: **66 POUNDS (30 KG)**

INTELLIGENCE
■■■■■■■□□□

AGILITY
■■■■■■■□□

STRENGTH
■■■■■■■□□□

ENDURANCE
■■■■■■■■□□

SPEED
■■■■■■□□□□

ATTACK
■■■■■■■■■□

FEARLESS FLIER

Hopelessly outmatched, flying fish are too small to outswim the giant ocean predators that chase them. They have only one means of escape, but it's effective. They accelerate underwater to speeds of up to 40 miles (65 km) per hour and head toward the sky. Bursting free, they vibrate their tails to taxi across the ocean's surface and take to the air, gliding up to one-quarter of a mile (400 m) before diving back into the sea.

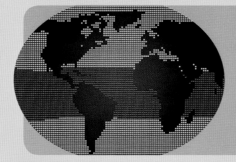

GEOGRAPHY
Tropical waters of the Indian, Atlantic, and Pacific oceans

HABITAT
Skims over waters 40 degrees north and south of the equator

FLYING FISH
Exocoetidae

LENGTH: **9 INCHES (23 CM)**   WEIGHT: **1 OUNCE (30 G)**

INTELLIGENCE	AGILITY
■■□■■■■■■■	■■■■■■■■■■

STRENGTH	ENDURANCE
■□■■■■■■■	■■■■■■■■■■

SPEED	EVASION
■■■■■□□□□□	■■■■■■■■□□

YELLOWFIN TUNA
Large open-water predators like yellowfin tuna eat flying fish. They try to leap after their flying prey, but they don't soar—they belly-flop!

ENEMY

TOOL TIME

AIR AND SEA WINGS
The two types of flying fish can be identified by the number of "wings" they have. The majority of flying fish have two pectoral fins, but some Atlantic species have four wide flying appendages.

HANG GLIDERS
Two wide pectoral fins open wide like birds' wings to let flying fish glide through the air and escape enemies.

SUPERPOWER
Long-distance jumping

EQUIPMENT
Pectoral "wing" fins; streamlined body; bifocal eyes

WEAKNESS
Able to change direction only while in water

FACT
Most flying fish don't actually fly. They jump high enough to catch an air current, then soar along it.

REAR BOOSTER
Flying fish vibrate their tails to lift out of the water. Repeated tail dips boost acceleration.

BIFOCAL LENS
Special cone-shaped structures inside flying fish eyes help them see clearly in water and air.

HIDDEN TREASURE
Flying fish protect their eggs from vicious predators by nesting in seaweed beds.

WHIPLASH

Two spines at the end of their tails inflict attackers with poison-laced puncture wounds.

MINESWEEPER

Rays glide close to the ground in order to locate and trap prey before grinding it in their powerful jaws.

SUPERPOWER
Stinging attack

EQUIPMENT
Wide pectoral fins; long tail; poisonous stingers

WEAKNESS
Periphery defenses (stingrays can only stab enemies swimming over their heads)

FACT
To protect mothers during birth, raylets are born with skin covering their barbed tails.

E-MAIL

Receptors in their noses allow stingrays to pick up electromagnetic signals sent by other rays and sea animals.

EXTENDABLE EYEBALLS

Rays' unusual eyes stretch forward on long stalks to enhance peripheral vision.

GEOGRAPHY
Tropical and warm seas of Africa, Australia, and Indonesia; Red Sea

HABITAT
Glides in sheltered bays and lagoons

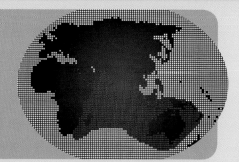

BARBED FLIER

Streamlined stingrays use their fins like wings to "fly" through the water. They may act shy, but when provoked, rays prove as dangerous as they are graceful and will lash out with their long whip tails. These tails are equipped with poison-coated barbs that slice cleanly into enemy flesh. Once embedded, the curved spines are impossible to remove without causing massive tissue damage to the victim.

ENEMY

HAMMERHEAD SHARKS
By pinning stingrays to the seabed with their skulls, hammerheads try to avoid the rays' painful stings while chowing down.

TOOL TIME

WHIP-TAIL WEAPON
Barbed ray tails are such effective defense weapons that people in Africa and Sri Lanka attach stingers to the ends of whips to create their own ray weaponry.

BLUE-SPOTTED STINGRAY
Taeniura lymma

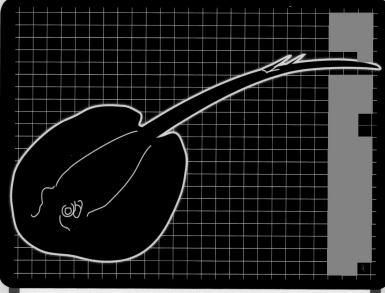

LENGTH: **10 INCHES (25 CM)**

INTELLIGENCE	AGILITY
■■■■■■■□□□	■■■■■■■■□□

STRENGTH	ENDURANCE
■■■■■□□□□□	■■■■■■□□□□

SPEED	ATTACK
■■■■■□□□□	■■■■■■■■■■

SULTANS OF SULFUR

Not your average earthworms, giant tubeworms rise from the ocean floor at heights of up to 8 feet (2.5 m), making these monstrous animals some of the largest invertebrates in the world. Despite their size, tubeworms are not hunters. They farm their food in hostile conditions near underwater volcanoes where temperatures vary from around 35 to 70°F (2–20°C).

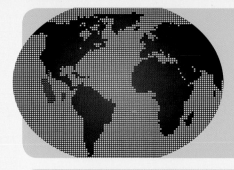

GEOGRAPHY
Eastern Pacific Rise, Galapagos Rift, and Guaymas Basin

HABITAT
Clings to the edges of volcanic deep-sea vents

GIANT TUBEWORM
Riftia pachyptila

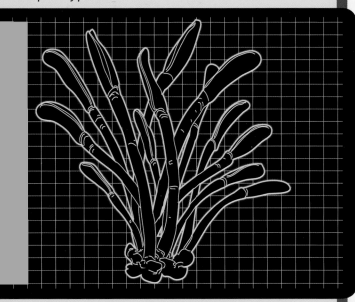

LENGTH: **5 FEET (1.5 M)** DIAMETER: **2 INCHES (5 CM)**

INTELLIGENCE
■▪■■■■■■■■

AGILITY
■■■■■■■■■■

STRENGTH
■ ■■■■■■■■

ENDURANCE
■■■■■■■■■■

SPEED

EVASION
■■■

FAIR TRADE
Giant tubeworms have no mouths or stomachs to digest food. Their blood-filled plumes house bacteria that absorb inedible chemicals, like sulfur, from the water. Bacteria change sulfur into sugars—the worms' food—and deliver it, via blood, to worms. In return, worms provide bacteria with needed shelter, oxygen, and carbon dioxide.

ANCHORS AWAY
Tubeworms are sealed at the bottom with a multitasking material that roots them in place.

SUPER STRETCH
Tubeworms get their surprising height by growing at least 5 inches (13 cm) a year, adding height at the roots of their bodies.

SUPERPOWER
Far-out farming

EQUIPMENT
Protective outer tube; plume; interior body; anchor

WEAKNESS
Dependent on bacteria for food

FACT
Giant tubeworm larvae hunt and move freely for forty days before setting anchor up to 60 miles (100 km) away.

TUBE SOCK
These soft worms secrete a material similar to insect shells, forming protective tubes around their squishy bodies.

DISAPPEARING ACT
A muscular organ can draw the worm's plume into its tube if it is attacked by crabs.

BONE CRUSHER
The large jaws of a killer whale are powerful enough to snap a captured seal or porpoise in half with a single bite.

SURROUND SOUND
By sending out clicking bursts and receiving echoes back through their jaws, orcas map out their surroundings.

PODCAST
Killer whales broadcast sounds to each other through an oil-filled portion of their skulls.

SUPERPOWERS
Team tactics; superintelligence

EQUIPMENT
Cone-shaped teeth; auditory communication

WEAKNESS
Slow development (takes up to six years before pups can hunt independently)

FACT
Killer whales produce sounds intense enough to stun or even kill distant prey.

KNOCKOUT PUNCH
Orcas herd herring into balls, then stun the fish by slapping them with their huge flukes before eating.

GEOGRAPHY

Arctic, Atlantic, Pacific, and Indian oceans

HABITAT

Hunts coastal beaches and deep cold waters along the high latitudes

KILLER PODS

Living up to ninety years and traveling in family groups called pods, killer whales, or orcas, form the roving gangs of the sea. Highly organized, they divide and conquer by splitting into efficient hunting groups. Their strong sense of order prevents fighting, too. When killer whale groups share waters, visiting and resident pods avoid competition by eating different foods, which means that everyone wins—except their prey.

PREY

GRAY WHALES

Orcas are actually large dolphins. They get their "killer" name because they hunt and kill whales, although they prefer to eat salmon.

IN ACTION

MAKING WAVES

Killer whales use their giant bodies to create waves large enough to drive seals up on shore for easy capture. They also use their wave-making skills to save other killer whales that are stranded on land.

KILLER WHALE
Orcinus orca

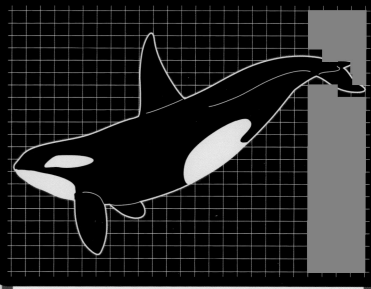

LENGTH: **30 FEET (9 M)**   WEIGHT: **4.5 TONS (4 TONNES)**

INTELLIGENCE
■■■■■■■■■

AGILITY
■■■■■■■■■

STRENGTH
■■■■■■■■■■

ENDURANCE
■■■■■■■■■■■

SPEED
■■■■■■■■■■

ATTACK
■■■■■■■■■

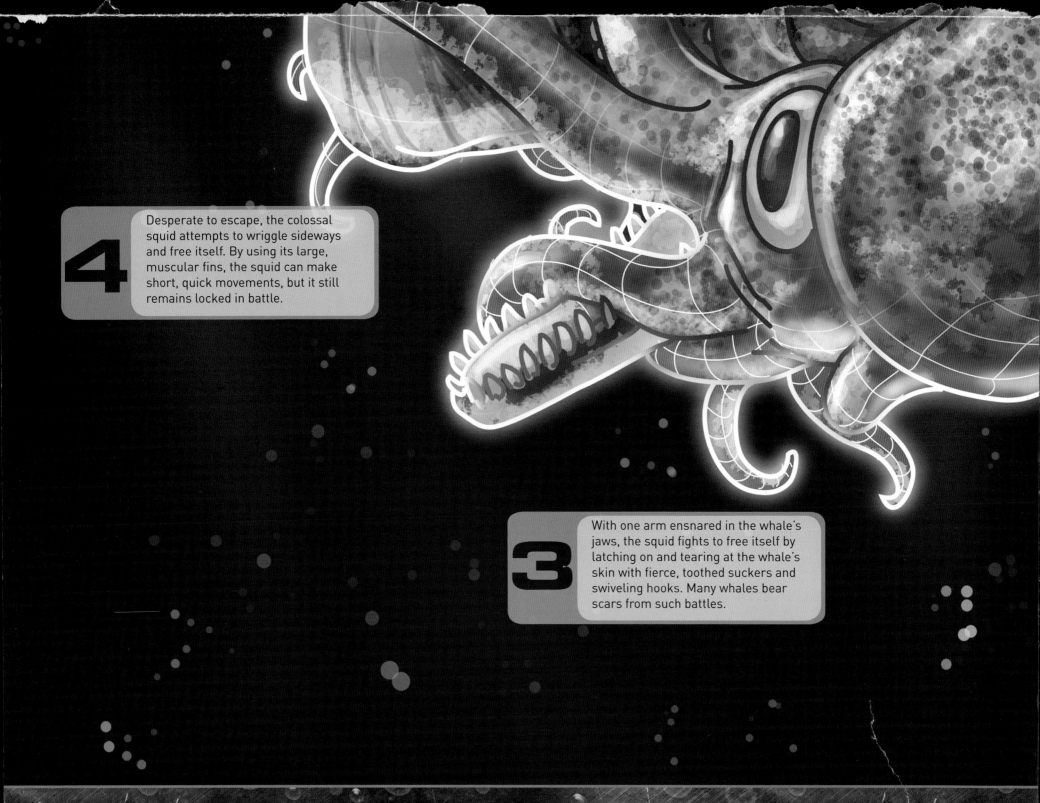

4 Desperate to escape, the colossal squid attempts to wriggle sideways and free itself. By using its large, muscular fins, the squid can make short, quick movements, but it still remains locked in battle.

3 With one arm ensnared in the whale's jaws, the squid fights to free itself by latching on and tearing at the whale's skin with fierce, toothed suckers and swiveling hooks. Many whales bear scars from such battles.

5 The whale may be four times larger than the squid, but the squid can breathe in water. After nearly an hour of submersion, the whale flexes its large fluke and speeds upward. At the surface, the squid, accustomed to the high pressure of the deep sea, struggles and finds escape difficult.

EVIL EYES

Colossal squid have forward-facing, soccer-ball-size eyes for tracking. Their huge orbs have glowing cell strips that work like headlights for hunting enemies in the dark.

THE SQUID AND THE WHALE

Matchups between sperm whales and colossal squid are a thing of mystery, though squid beaks and tentacle hooks have been found in whales' stomachs, and scars have been seen on their skin—proof positive of squid battles! Sperm whales also lurk near trenches where squid live, looking for a tentacle snack—and maybe a fight.

JET PROPULSION

The huge squid fills its gigantic mantle **1**, which can measure up to 8 feet (2.5 m) long, with water. The squid then forces the liquid out through an opening on its underside **2** to propel itself through the sea at top speed.

SHARP-TONGUED

Beyond the squid's sharp beak lies the tooth-covered, tonguelike radula.

SIZE COMPARISON

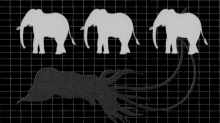

The colossal squid is the world's largest known squid. The only complete specimen measures 14 feet (4 m) long—that's about the same length as two male African elephants!

SUPER SUCKERS

Rows of twenty to twenty-five hooks line the ends of the colossal squid's two club-shaped arms. Each hook swivels a full 360 degrees to hold fast to struggling prey.

GIANT BRAIN

Sperm whales' colossal brains weigh as much as a car tire—17 pounds (8 kg). They are topped by oil-filled bulges that amplify sound waves made by the whale to stun prey. The oil also aids diving. Whales can drag foes to depths of 6,500 feet (2,000 m).

OUTBOARD MOTOR

When pursued, whales use huge flukes to swim up to 25 miles (40 km) per hour.

MEGA TEETH

Whales' thirty-six to fifty teeth grow on its lower jaws. Each tooth can grow up to 8 inches (20 cm) long and weigh 2 pounds (1 kg), and each fits into its own socket in the upper jaw.

SIZE COMPARISON

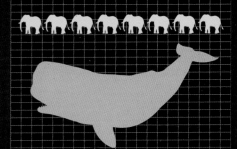

Sperm whales are the largest toothed hunters in the sea. They can reach lengths up to 60 feet (18 m) and weigh as much as 60 tons (55 tonnes).

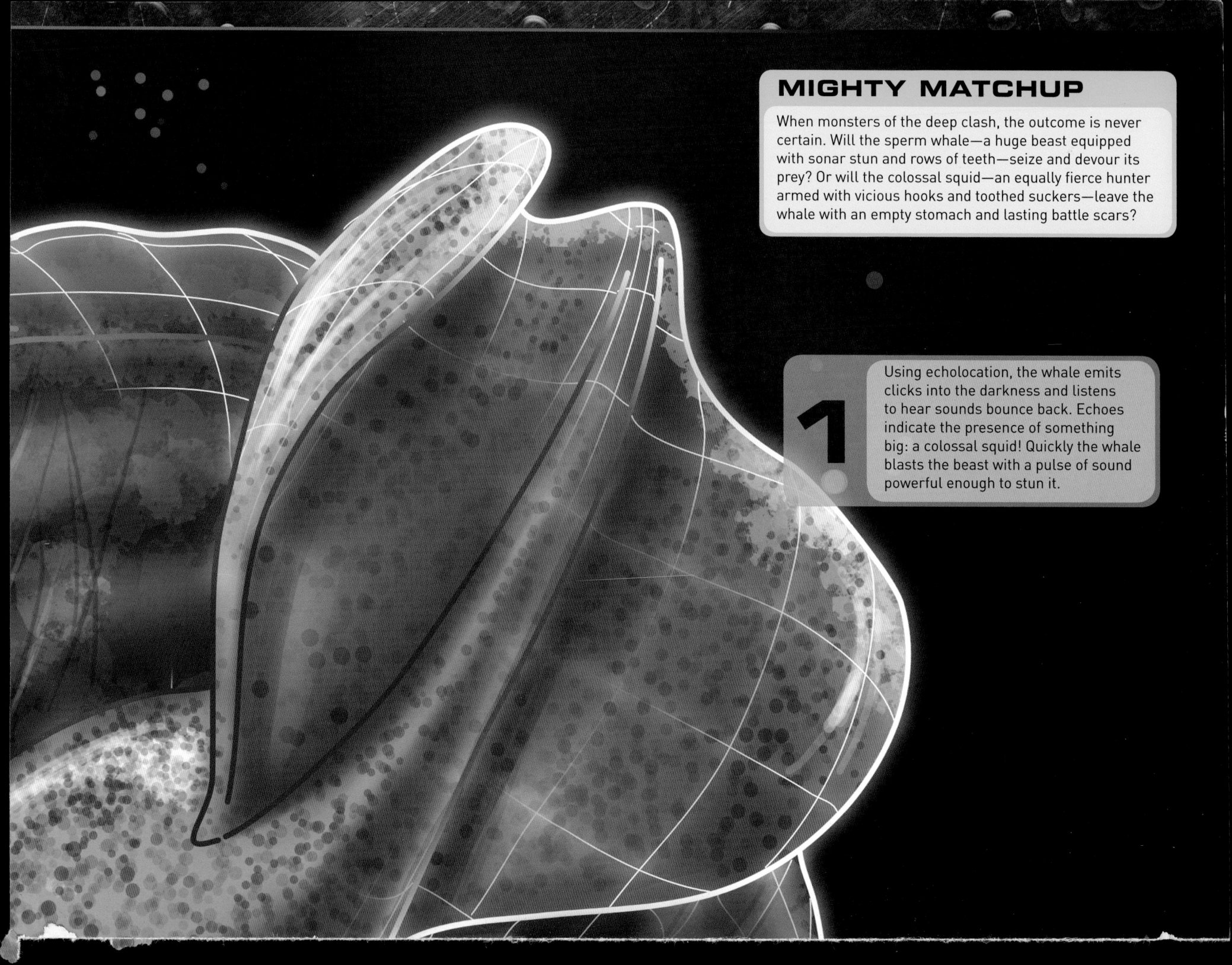

MIGHTY MATCHUP

When monsters of the deep clash, the outcome is never certain. Will the sperm whale—a huge beast equipped with sonar stun and rows of teeth—seize and devour its prey? Or will the colossal squid—an equally fierce hunter armed with vicious hooks and toothed suckers—leave the whale with an empty stomach and lasting battle scars?

1 Using echolocation, the whale emits clicks into the darkness and listens to hear sounds bounce back. Echoes indicate the presence of something big: a colossal squid! Quickly the whale blasts the beast with a pulse of sound powerful enough to stun it.

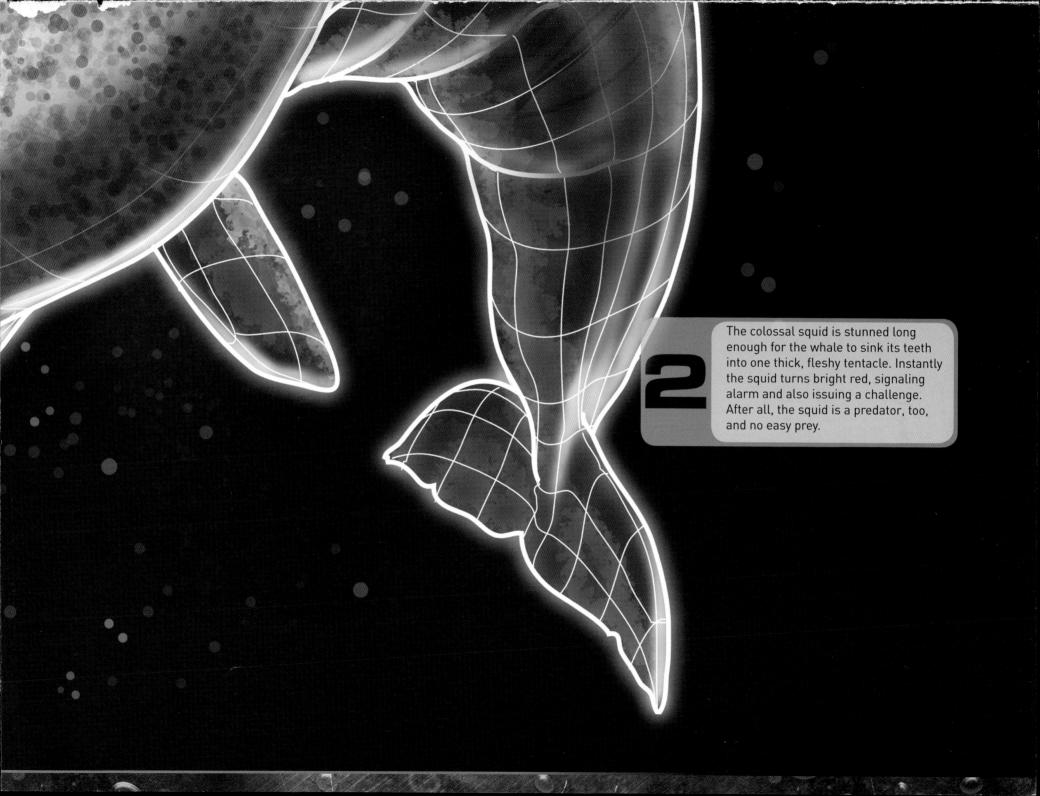

2 The colossal squid is stunned long enough for the whale to sink its teeth into one thick, fleshy tentacle. Instantly the squid turns bright red, signaling alarm and also issuing a challenge. After all, the squid is a predator, too, and no easy prey.

GLOSSARY

algae Plantlike organisms that most often grow in water. Algae are the base for most aquatic food chains, providing food for fish.

ally An animal that helps another animal, usually to the mutual benefit of both.

amphibious Able to live on land and in water.

appendage A projecting part of a larger plant or animal, such as an antenna, leg, or arm.

bay An inlet or smaller body of water set off from a main body of water. Bays often have calmer waters than open oceans and offer protected habitats.

bifocal Having the ability to focus vision at two different lengths. Special eye cones give flying fish bifocal ability and allow them to see in the air and underwater.

bioluminescent Producing its own light as a living organism, usually using bacteria. Deep-sea fish frequently produce light to attract other fish as food, mates, or as a means of communication.

blubber A layer of fat. Whales and seals have layers of blubber that work to insulate and keep them warm in icy waters.

buoyancy The tendency of a body to float in water. Some sea animals control their buoyancy by increasing or decreasing the amount of air in their bodies.

calcify To make or become hard and stony due to deposited calcium salts. The process of calcification gives sea stars and coral their bony exteriors.

camouflage A physical characteristic that helps an animal blend into its environment.

carapace A bony and hard case that covers the back of an animal. A turtle's shell is an example of a carapace.

circulatory system The system of heart and valves that circulates blood and lymph throughout the body, bringing oxygen and flushing waste. The crown-of-thorns sea star's circulatory system uses water instead of blood.

colony A population of animals living together usually for the good of all. In man-of-war colonies, each member helps by performing specific tasks for the benefit of the group.

copepods Tiny, shrimplike crustaceans that live in both freshwater and saltwater.

coral A rocklike deposit made up of the calcified skeletons of soft-bodied marine animals. Coral formations can grow into large reefs or islands; they provide a habitat for many undersea creatures.

crevice A narrow opening or crack. Coral reefs are filled with small crevices, perfect for fish and other aquatic life to live or hide in.

crustacean A large class of aquatic arthropods such as shrimp and crabs. Crustaceans have external skeletons, segmented bodies, jointed legs, and two pairs of antennae.

dermal denticles Hard, arrow-shaped outgrowths that cover skin and are similar in structure to teeth. Sharks' dermal denticles lay flat and increase their swimming efficiency.

dormant Temporarily inactive, or unused, but capable of being activated. Sea kraits have two lungs, one of which is largely dormant while the other is in use.

electromagnetism Magnetic attraction and repulsion created by a current of electricity.

enemy An animal that is harmful or has a negative relationship with another animal.

fin A thin appendage on the outside of an aquatic animal, such as a fish, that is used for propelling or guiding the body.

forage To search for and gather food.

fused Rigidly joined. If vertebrae (the individual bones of the spine) are fused, they act as one single bone, reducing flexibility.

gill An organ used by fish and many amphibians to obtain oxygen from water.

habitat The environment where an animal is best suited to live in the wild.

incubate To hatch eggs through warmth.

ink Liquid pigment, or color. Octopuses' ink is made of melanin, the same pigment humans have in their skin.

invertebrate An animal lacking a backbone.

kelp Any of various large brown seaweed.

krill Small crustaceans and their larvae. Krill are the primary food source for many aquatic fish and mammals such as whales.

lagoon A shallow pond or body of salty water near or connected to a larger body of water.

liver A large vital organ in vertebrates and other animals that performs many functions, including detoxification (the production of chemicals necessary for digestion) and the synthesizing of protein.

lure A decoy used to attract other animals. Anglerfish have glowing lures that attract prey.

mollusk Any of a large group of invertebrate animals (animals lacking backbones) with soft, unsegmented bodies, usually encased in shells. Clams and octopuses are mollusks.

morph Short for metamorphose, meaning to change in form.

navigate To steer or control one's course.

ocean The whole body of saltwater that covers nearly three-fourths of Earth.

paralysis The complete or partial loss of function, especially movement or sensation, in a part of the body.

pectoral fins A pair of front fins, one on each side, situated behind the head of a fish.

peripheral The outer edges of an animal's range of vision. Stingrays' long eye stalks give them a wider range of peripheral vision.

phytoplankton Tiny plant life that floats in water. Phytoplankton swarms make water appear cloudy and provide the base for many food chains. For instance, phytoplankton are fed on by krill, which in turn are fed on by baleen whales.

polyp The young form of an animal, such as an anemone or coral. It has a cylinder-shaped body that is anchored at one end and has a mouth opening surrounded by tentacles at the other end.

pores Small openings in the skin.

predator An animal that hunts and eats other animals.

prehistoric Existing before the time of recorded human history. Horseshoe crabs have been around for more than 350 million years, predating humans.

prey Animals that are hunted and eaten by other animals.

receptors A cell or group of cells that receive stimuli and work like sense organs.

reef A chain or ridge of rocks, coral, or sand near the surface of the water. Reefs are popular habitats for eels and sea dragons.

reflexive Behavior that occurs automatically, without thinking. An octopus's reflexive tentacles reach out and grab objects without directions to do so from its brain.

regeneration Regrowth or replacement of body, parts or whole, by the growth of new tissue. If a sea star's limb is separated from its body, the limb can regenerate into a new body.

respiratory Having to do with breathing, the physical act or system whereby an animal gets the oxygen it needs to survive.

sea lice Tiny crustacean parasites that live on fish and other marine animals.

subtropical The geographical regions bordering the tropical zone between 20 and 40 degrees in both latitudes. The subtropical regions are characterized by warm winters and hot summers.

temperate Associated with mild climates, weather, or temperatures. Such regions make comfortable homes.

tentacles Long, flexible structures that stick out, usually around the head or mouth, of an animal. Portuguese man-of-wars and octopuses use tentacles for grasping prey.

tolerance The ability to withstand something toxic or unpleasant. Moray eels can build up tolerance to sea krait poison and survive single bites. Multiple bites may still be lethal.

tropical The geographical region between the latitudes 23.5 degrees north and south of the equator. The tropical oceans are characterized by warm waters that usually exceed 68°F (20°C) and stay constant throughout the year.

ultraviolet Light waves situated beyond the spectrum visible to humans on the violet end. One of horseshoe crabs' five sets of eyes can detect ultraviolet light.

vaccines A preparation of microbes that is introduced (as a shot or injection) to produce or increase immunity to a particular disease. Horseshoe crab blood is used to test vaccines and ensure that they are not contaminated.

venom A poisonous substance produced by sea kraits, lionfish, and some other water creatures that can be injected into the tissue of prey to paralyze or kill.

CREDITS

All illustrations by **Liberum Donum** (Juan Calle, Santiago Calle, Andres Penagos).

All images courtesy of **Shutterstock** unless noted below.
Alamy: 37 main
Image Quest Marine: 7 top far right (Peter Batson); 13 main (Jez Tryner); 28 main (Peter Batson); 36 bottom (Peter Parks); 40 bottom (Peter Batson)
iStock: 6 bottom far left; 12 bottom; 14 main; 24 main; 25 top; 30 bottom; 34 main; 36 top
National Geographic Image Collection: 27 main (Paul Nicklen); 41 main (Emory Kristof)
Minden Pictures: 17 bottom far right (Norbert Wu); 18 bottom (Norbert Wu); 19 main (Norbert Wu); 31 main (Georgette Douwma); 42 main (Hiroya Minakuchi); 43 bottom (Hiroya Minakuchi)
National Oceanic and Atmospheric Administration: 17 top far left (Bodil Bluhm); 17 bottom far left; 17 bottom left; 17 top right and 17 top far right (Kevin Raskoff)

ACKNOWLEDGMENTS

Special thanks to Jacqueline Aaron, Karen Clarke, Bret Hansen, Sheila Masson, Susan McCombs, and Marisa Solís.